The First Woman of Medicine —
The Story of Elizabeth Blackwell

by Scott Matthew
Illustrated by Wayne Atkinson
Cover illustration by Denis Orloff

Copyright© 1978 by Contemporary Perspectives, Inc.
All rights reserved. No part of this book may be reproduced
or utilized in any form or by any means, electronic or mechanical,
including photocopying, recording, or by any information storage
and retrieval system, without permission in writing from the
Distributor and the Publisher. Inquiries should be addressed
to the DISTRIBUTOR: Silver Burdett Company, Morristown, New
Jersey 07960 and the PUBLISHER: Contemporary Perspectives, Inc.,
223 East 48th Street, New York, New York 10017.

Library of Congress Number: 78-16305

Library of Congress Cataloging in Publication Data

> Matthew, Scott, 1934-
> The first woman of medicine: The story of Elizabeth Blackwell
>
> SUMMARY: Presents the career of Elizabeth Blackwell
> stressing the problems she had to overcome to be a doctor,
> an all-male profession in the mid-nineteenth century.
> 1. Blackwell, Elizabeth, 1821-1910 — Juvenile literature.
> 2. Physicians — New York (State) — Biography — Juvenile litera-
> ture. 3. Physicians — England — Biography — Juvenile literature.
> 4. Women physicians — New York (State) — Biography — Juvenile
> literature. 5. Women physicians — England — Biography —
> Juvenile literature. [1. Blackwell, Elizabeth, 1821-1910.
> 2. Women physicians. 3. Physicians] I. Atkinson, Wayne.
> II. Title.
> R154.B623R44   610'.92'4 [B] [92]   78-16305
> ISBN 0-89547-042-X

Manufactured in the United States of America
ISBN 0-89547-042-X

Contents

Chapter 1
    The Letter   5

Chapter 2
    Sam Blackwell Speaks Out   11

Chapter 3
    A New Dream   15

Chapter 4
    The Joke That Backfired   25

Chapter 5
    Is Everything Lost?   36

Chapter 6
    The Final Dream   43

The Letter

The clock in the hall struck ten. Elizabeth Blackwell had been up since six in the morning. She could not sleep. Where on earth was that mailman? He should have been here an hour ago! The young woman had looked out the window a hundred times. Still there was no sign of Mr. Reed. Elizabeth was sure he would have the letter for her today.

"I can't just sit here any more," Elizabeth said to the empty room. She put on her long black coat. She raced out the front door. "If Mr. Reed won't come to me, I'll find him!" Down the street she went, half running, half walking. Her eyes skipped from house to house. Mr. Reed was not to be found. "A mailman has to be *somewhere* at ten in the morning," she said. And she looked behind her as she turned the corner.

Elizabeth ran right into Mr. Reed. His mailbag went flying. "What's the big rush, Miss Elizabeth?" the old man cried. He got up and brushed his coat.

"Oh, Mr. Reed, I *am* sorry! I wasn't looking — I mean I was looking for — Mr. Reed, do you have the letter? I can't wait another second!"

The old man kept brushing his coat. His face looked angry. But his eyes were smiling. Mr. Reed liked Elizabeth Blackwell. He had the letter she wanted, and he knew it. "Now let's see," Mr. Reed said. He looked at all the letters he had picked up from the ground. "Here's one for the Reverend Mr. and Mrs. Dickson. You can bring that home to them. Save me a trip." Mr. Reed couldn't help but smile as he looked at poor Elizabeth's face.

"Oh, and here's one for you. It's from your sister Emily. Here's another for you. It's from your brother." Elizabeth took the letters from him. Sadly, she turned to go back home. Slowly Mr. Reed took one more letter from his bag. "Oh, Elizabeth, I almost forgot. Here's one more for you. It's from a Dr. Warrington."

"Dr. Warrington!" Elizabeth almost knocked the mailman down again. "Oh, Mr. Reed, that's it. That's the one!" She pulled the letter from him. It had come from Philadelphia. Elizabeth ran back home. She wanted to be alone when she read the letter. *This could be the biggest moment in her 25-year-old life!*

Elizabeth lived with the Reverend Mr. and Mrs. Dickson. She was a teacher at their school in North Carolina. When Elizabeth reached the house, Mrs. Dickson was dusting. Elizabeth rushed past her. She was halfway up the stairs when Mrs. Dickson called to her. "Is it the letter, Elizabeth? What did Dr. Warrington say? Are you going?"

Elizabeth tore open the letter. She began to read. Mrs. Dickson didn't need to ask what it said. She could almost read the letter in Elizabeth's face. The smile was gone from her lips. The light was no longer in her eyes. "They don't want me, Mrs. Dickson. Just because I am a woman I can't go to their school. I'll never be a doctor!"

Mrs. Dickson took the letter from her young friend's hand. The last few lines told her why Elizabeth was so upset.

You see, Miss Blackwell, this is 1846. The world is not ready for women to become doctors. I know from your letters how much you want to be a doctor. There is only one way I can have you in my class. You will have to agree to dress and act like a man. No one can know we have a woman in our school.

But I ask you once again, Miss Blackwell: Why not do what other smart women do? Become a nurse and let the men be doctors.

Elizabeth couldn't believe it. How could people be so mean? She was smart and ready to work hard. Why couldn't she be anything she wanted? Who said only men could be doctors?

"Mrs. Dickson, I am not going to cut my hair short. I am not going to dress like a man. But I *am* going to be a doctor."

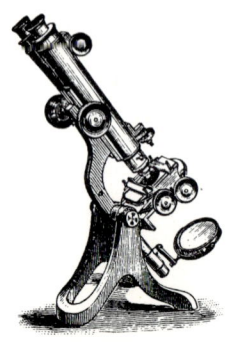

Sam Blackwell Speaks Out

Elizabeth Blackwell was born in Bristol, England, on February 3, 1821. Her father, Samuel, was a good man. But he had ideas that made his friends worry about him. For one thing, he didn't want slaves to do his work. Mr. Blackwell was in the sugar business. Everyone else in the sugar business owned slaves. But Samuel Blackwell thought all men and women should be paid for their work. He had other ideas as well.

"All people are the same, Aunt Bar. That means black and white, rich and poor. It also means men and women!" Elizabeth was walking past the living room. She heard her father's angry words. They stopped her in her tracks. She had never heard her father talk this way to Aunt Bar before. Silently, she crept behind the sofa. She wanted to hear more.

"The way you treat your daughters is shameful, Samuel!" Aunt Bar's voice shook with anger. "Little girls must learn to cook and sew. They must be taught to be wives and mothers. It is wrong to teach them that they are just like boys."

"Their bodies are different, Aunt Bar. But their minds are the same. When my daughters grow up, they will cook and sew — if they want to. But they will also be able to do men's work if they want to. They will know enough to make a choice!"

"You are wasting your money on their schooling, Samuel. You are filling their heads with silly dreams. Dreams of things that will never be."

Elizabeth could hardly control her anger. Her aunt was wrong! She wanted to jump up and tell her so. She loved school. She loved growing up just like her brothers.

"Don't keep telling people about your foolish ideas, Samuel. They are afraid of you. You will be left with nothing." Aunt Bar's voice interrupted Elizabeth's thoughts. "You are losing your friends and your good name."

"My daughters are more important to me than either." Elizabeth would remember these words for a long time. She was proud of her father. But she knew that his ideas frightened many people. And they hurt business. It was getting harder for the Blackwells to live in Bristol.

In 1832 Samuel Blackwell sold his house and his sugar company. The family set sail for the United States. Samuel believed America would mean freedom for *all* his children.

A New Dream

It would be a long time before Samuel Blackwell's dreams of America came true. For six years the family searched for a home. First they tried New York, then Boston and Chicago.

Finally the Blackwells moved to Cincinnati, Ohio. There they found a home. Within a short time, there was a Samuel Blackwell Sugar Company. It was like the one in Bristol. He knew the sugar business, and his company did well.

Samuel Blackwell began to make money. It was not a lot. But it was enough to send his children to private schools. Things began to look up. But to her parents' surprise, this good fortune made Elizabeth unhappy. "It is just not fair!" Elizabeth explained to her father.

"We have so much more than other people. I want to do something to help the poor. I don't know what I will do. I just know I *must* help."

"You will," her father told her. "But you must be patient. Just wait a little longer. As soon as I save enough money, I will help you. You see, I believe in your dream too." Samuel Blackwell's promise never came true. He died suddenly that year. He left his family with a lot of hope, but only $25.00 in the bank. All at once the Blackwells were poor.

Mrs. Blackwell had nine children and a big house to take care of. She had to find a way to earn money. The thing she knew best was teaching. She had spent many years helping her own children with their lessons. Could she now help other children? And make money at the same time? She turned the big house into a school. It was called the Blackwell Boarding School for Girls. Each of the children had a job at the school. Elizabeth became a teacher.

The boarding school was a success. Elizabeth enjoyed teaching very much. But soon her unhappy feelings returned. She dreamed of helping the poor. That is what her father would have wanted. She knew she had to leave home. She knew her mother would understand.

In 1845, Elizabeth, now 24 years old, moved to Kentucky. She would teach in a school for very poor children. As soon as she arrived, she saw how really important a teacher could be. She spent long hours with her pupils. She grew to like them very much.

But many of the children were sick. She could teach them to read and write. But she could not make them feel better. She could not make them well. Only a doctor could do that. "If only I could be a doctor," thought Elizabeth.

She talked about her wish with Mary Donaldson. Mary was her best friend. "Maybe you can," Mary said. She had a broad smile on her face. But Elizabeth knew that Mary was very serious. "Just imagine. You would be Dr. Elizabeth Blackwell. You would be the first woman doctor in America."

Over the next few months, Elizabeth and Mary talked a lot. Mary was sure that Elizabeth could be a doctor if she really wanted to. Slowly, Elizabeth started to believe the dream herself.

Neither woman knew that Mary would be treated by doctors herself in a short time. She was dying of cancer.

Just before she died, Mary called Elizabeth to her bedside. "Become a doctor — for me," Mary whispered. Her voice was very weak. Elizabeth could hardly hear her. She bent close to her dying friend.

"Elizabeth, I have suffered so much. There are some things men just can't understand about women's illnesses. I wish I had been treated by a woman."

Elizabeth would never forget Mary's last words. Mary had believed in Elizabeth. She believed that her friend could become a doctor if she really wanted to. But did Elizabeth really want to? That is what she had to decide.

Elizabeth thought about women like Mary. They needed women doctors. She thought about her father's dreams for her. She would do it! No matter what it took, she would be the first woman doctor! Maybe it was lucky that Elizabeth did not know then how hard it would be to become a doctor. She might never have tried.

Elizabeth's struggle to become a doctor started right away. She needed money for medical school. She had to find a job that would pay more — a lot more. She didn't want to leave her pupils. But she had no choice. Maybe one day she would come back to them as a doctor. Then she might help them even more.

Elizabeth's search for a new job did not take long. She heard that a Reverend Mr. Dickson in North Carolina needed a teacher for his school. The pay was very good. So Elizabeth wrote to him. In her letter she told him how she felt about children and teaching. Within a few days she received an answer. Her eyes skipped quickly to the last lines. They told her just what she wanted to hear:

Elizabeth wrote to Mr. Dickson in North Carolina.

There is a place for you in our school. Please come as soon as you can. We have an extra bedroom in our home. If you like, you can live with us.

Things were starting to fall into place. At least they *seemed* to be. She was very happy living with the Dicksons. And she was earning money to pay for medical school. But then Dr. Warrington's letter came.

The letter made Elizabeth very unhappy. It seemed that she would not be a doctor after all. But then she decided to try again. She would *not* be a nurse, she *would* become a doctor. She wrote more letters to other medical schools. She would find another school. She was sure. "I am as good as any man." She would say those words over and over for a long time to come.

The Joke
That Backfired

One of Elizabeth's letters went to Dr. Allen. He was the head of the Philadelphia School of Anatomy. He knew a lot of important people. Maybe he would write to them for her. It was worth taking a chance.

Dr. Allen wrote back a few weeks later. To Elizabeth's surprise, he asked her to come to the school. He would see her at twelve o'clock sharp on August 28, 1846.

Dr. Allen wanted to see just what kind of woman Elizabeth Blackwell was. He would tell her what being a doctor was all about. That would change her mind.

"Do you know what medical school means?" he asked Elizabeth. "As a woman you will be bothered by

25

the study of the body." Elizabeth almost laughed. How could he say such a thing? Why would anyone's body bother her?

"Why don't you come back at eight o'clock? You can see what I mean," Dr. Allen said. He seemed to be hiding a smile.

Elizabeth arrived at the lab right on time. She wondered what Dr. Allen would show her. She didn't have to wait long. A smiling Dr. Allen came in a few minutes later. Elizabeth felt he was up to something. Did it have something to do with the large black box he was carrying?

Dr. Allen put the box down on the table. "Come here, Miss Blackwell. This box may help you decide if you really want to become a doctor." He opened the box, and Elizabeth's eyes opened wide. It was an arm — no body, just an arm!

She almost fell over at the sight! The arm was yellow. *Wrinkled.* Just the smell of it almost knocked her down. Dr. Allen knew he had surprised her. But he gave her no time to catch her breath. He quickly pointed to a spot on the arm. "Here," he said, "we will make a cut here. We have to open up all the skin. Then we can see the muscle. Are you ready, Miss Blackwell? Or shall we call the whole thing off?"

"Ready," Elizabeth said. Her voice was strong. But she didn't feel very strong. She watched closely. Dr. Allen cut the arm. He showed her the muscle hidden within.

Dr. Allen looked at Elizabeth. This woman was brave! Could he have been wrong? *Could* a woman be a doctor?

They talked for hours, about the arm and about Elizabeth's dream. Elizabeth wondered — had she changed Dr. Allen's mind? She knew she had when he promised to help her find a medical school.

He gave her many names. She wrote to everyone. Within a week she heard from all but one. No one wanted her. They would not have a woman in their schools.

Only one school was left. It was several weeks before the letter came. Elizabeth didn't even get excited. She was sure it would say the same thing as all the others. But when Elizabeth finally did read the letter, she read it over and over again.

> We, the students of the Geneva Medical School, want you to join our class. America is the land of freedom for all people. We want you to go to

Elizabeth watched closely as Dr. Allen cut the arm.

medical school with us. We want the first woman doctor to be a graduate of Geneva.

Elizabeth didn't believe her eyes. Could this be true? Were they really taking her? It was true, but there was no way Elizabeth could know what had happened. The head of the Geneva Medical School in New York had left the choice up to the students. They were all men. And they had agreed to give her a chance.

Even the head of the school didn't know why the students had voted to take Elizabeth. The students thought it was all a big joke. They *knew* that a woman could never be a doctor. But it would be funny to watch one try.

Elizabeth had her work cut out for her. She had to change their minds. And she was sure she could do it. She would study more than any other student. She would get better marks than anyone else. Her work paid off. She rose to near the top of her class.

At first the men in the school could not believe it. Elizabeth was not like any woman they had ever met. They began to wonder if she might not become a very good doctor. Certainly they were growing to like her very much.

But not all her teachers felt as warmly toward Elizabeth. There was Dr. Webster for one. He hated

Elizabeth worked hard to be one of the best students in her class.

having her in his classes. One day he was to teach a class on childbirth and the woman's body. Before starting, he asked Elizabeth to leave the room. "Miss Blackwell," he said, "this class is not for you. It will only bother you. And it will bother the men. Please stay out until we finish."

Elizabeth could not believe her ears. She asked to stay. How else could she become a doctor? Dr. Webster said no. So Elizabeth asked if he would let the other students vote on it. Did they think childbirth was for men only? Once again, the men were all for Elizabeth. When the vote was in, all the students stood and cheered her. Dr. Webster didn't cheer. But Elizabeth learned what she needed to know about bringing babies into the world.

If Elizabeth Blackwell thought medical school was a problem, she would find the world outside school much harder. A student had to work at a hospital before becoming a doctor. No hospital would let her train. If no hospital would let her train, where could she go? There was only one choice — The Blockley Almshouse. It was a hospital for the very poor.

Elizabeth was sick over what she saw at Blockley. For one thing, the windows were never opened. The smell inside was terrible. For another, rats ran up and down the halls. They stole what little food there was.

The poor children had no place to run and play. They were dirty and poorly fed and thin.

Elizabeth wanted to change everything about Blockley. But Elizabeth had a much greater problem as well. No one would let her treat them. They wanted only a man to be their doctor. Elizabeth was looked upon as a nurse. She could change beds, but she could not touch anyone. Once again Elizabeth was turned away.

She went back to school for her final classes. It made her sad that people at Blockley would not let her help. But now medical school was coming to an end. She would soon be *Dr. Elizabeth Blackwell.* Then nothing could stop her.

5

Is Everything Lost?

"Miss Blackwell. I am glad you are here." Dr. Arnold, head of the Geneva Medical School, asked Elizabeth to sit down. He certainly seemed on edge.

"Your message sounded important, Dr. Arnold. I got here as soon as I could. I was just putting my things together. I'm leaving school right after graduation."

"That's what I — that is — " Dr. Arnold interrupted. "Miss Blackwell, I went along with the students. They wanted you to go to school here. But now I must say — that is — Miss Blackwell, you cannot graduate as a doctor. It is not the work of a woman."

Elizabeth had to convince
Dr. Arnold to change his mind.

Elizabeth didn't know what to say. This was the final blow. Years of hard work and now to hear *this*! How could Dr. Arnold do this to her? Suddenly, something she had said years ago to Mrs. Dickson came racing back to her: "I have never been as sure of anything in my life. I want to help the sick. I know I can because I am as good as any man."

Before she knew it, the words sprang from her mouth. Now that she had said them, she had to go on. She had to make Dr. Arnold change his mind. It took hours, but Elizabeth finally won.

On January 23, 1849, Elizabeth Blackwell became a doctor. And, of course, now she would face more problems. What would she do? Where would she go? Which hospital would take her?

Elizabeth was sure that no hospital in America would have her work with them. But, as always, she tried them all — just in case. And she was right. She would have to go to another country. She didn't care, but she was going to work as a doctor!

She found a hospital in Paris, France. It was called La Maternité. Women came there to give birth to their babies. Elizabeth loved the work. The part she liked most was watching operations. She wanted to become a surgeon. But it was only a dream. Women

One day while working in the laboratory...

didn't become surgeons. Then she remembered her other dreams. They had come true. Why not this one? She would try. But, in one bad moment, that dream would soon be broken for all time.

...Elizabeth burned her eyes with a strong medicine.

One day Elizabeth splashed a strong medicine in her eyes. She was in great pain. For three days and nights, Elizabeth could not open her eyes. The doctors were afraid she might not live. They felt their only chance to save her life was to take out her left eye. They put a glass eye in its place — an eye that would never see. Elizabeth would never be a surgeon.

For the first time in her life, Elizabeth gave up. She was now a doctor with only one eye. Who would ever want her help? She did not want to live. She would eat nothing, drink nothing. The doctors sent for her sister Emily.

"How can you act this way, Elizabeth? The Blackwells never give up at anything. How can you do this? Father would never forgive you."

"Leave me alone. I have nothing left," Elizabeth answered. Tears ran down her face.

"You have lost an eye. But everything else is the same. You are still a doctor. And you can help me. I am going to be the second woman doctor in America. But I am not as strong as you. I need you to help me."

"I don't understand. Why would you want to be a doctor? You know how hard it has been for me."

"Because I want to help the sick. Just like you." Emily knew her sister. Elizabeth might not want to live for her own dream. But she would do just about anything for someone else.

CHILDR[EN'S]
WAR[D]

6

The Final Dream

Over the next year, Elizabeth worked in St. Bartholomew's Hospital in London. Each day her right eye grew stronger. It became almost as strong as her new will to live.

"It is hard to believe that you were about to give up," Emily said to Elizabeth. It was a year after the accident. Emily knew that Elizabeth was pleased with herself that day. She had just saved the life of a little boy.

"When I think about lying in the hospital like that — well, it wasn't me — it was another person. I will never give up again. Emily, there is something I have wanted to talk to you about for a long time."

"I know. You want to go home," Emily interrupted.

"You should be a mind reader, not a doctor," Elizabeth said. She smiled at her sister. "I love England. But I must work in America. I have to go back."

Elizabeth returned to New York. She wanted to be a doctor there. But nothing had changed. There was still no hospital that would take her. She would have to open her own office. But how could she let people know about it? The only way was to put an ad in the newspaper. No doctor had ever done this before. But Elizabeth was not just any doctor.

> **DOCTOR OPENS OFFICE**
> Dr. Elizabeth Blackwell is pleased to announce the opening of her office at 44 University Place, New York City. Dr. Blackwell is a graduate of Geneva Medical School. She has trained for two years at La Maternité in Paris and St. Bartholomew's in London.

Not one person came to her door. Was there no one in New York who would see a woman doctor? She soon had to close her office.

But Elizabeth had to earn money. She started giving talks in churches and schools. She talked about

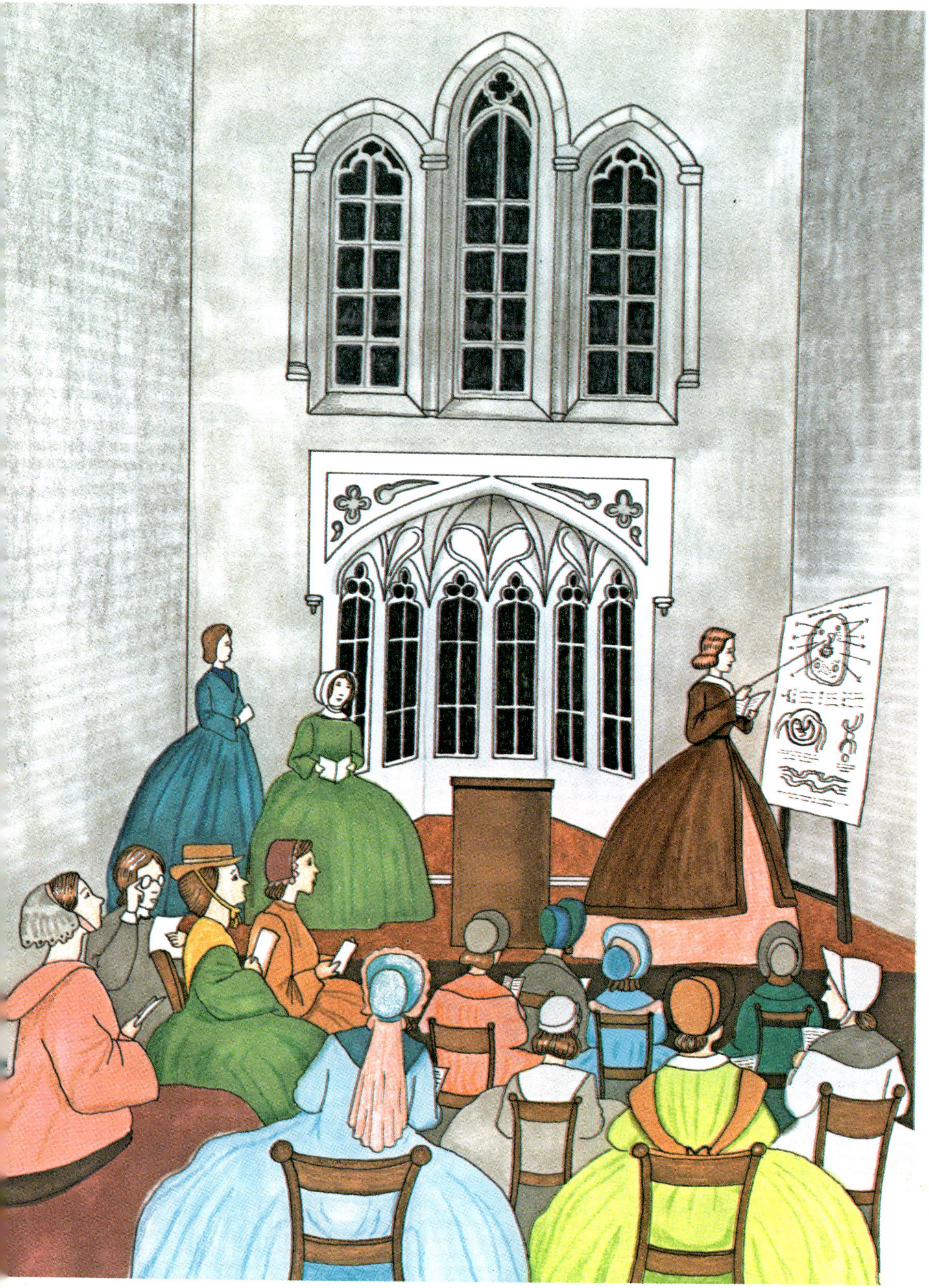

the rights of women. She talked about childbirth. Hundreds of women came to the meetings. Elizabeth told them things they had never heard before.

Elizabeth had one dream left. She wanted to open a hospital for poor women. It was something that no one had ever done before. With the money she earned from her talks she would try to make this last dream come true.

In 1853, Elizabeth opened the first hospital run by women — for women. It was called the New York Dispensary. The women who came there were too poor to go anywhere else. And the children who came there were those no one else cared about.

Now Emily too was a doctor. She joined her sister and became the hospital's first surgeon. The Blackwell sisters tried hard to care for the poor. But there were just too many. They needed another doctor. Elizabeth heard of a Polish doctor named Marie Zakrzewska. She had just come to America. Would she join them?

Marie not only joined the sisters, but the three women were soon able to open a larger hospital. In 1857 the three doctors opened the New York Infirmary for Women and Children. Elizabeth was too busy to think about anything other than her work. She and

In 1853 Elizabeth was able to open the first hospital for women.

everyone else at the Infirmary worked very hard to care for the sick.

The years passed quickly. One day Elizabeth knew how much she missed England. While she was helping others who were sick, she herself had not been well. Elizabeth decided to return to England. Many important people had now heard of Dr. Elizabeth Blackwell. In 1874 she was given an important job at the London School of Medicine for Women. But Elizabeth was ill. In 1879 she left her job to live in Hastings, where she spent the rest of her life. On May 31, 1910, Elizabeth Blackwell died.

Dr. Elizabeth Blackwell is remembered for her dreams: to strengthen the rights of women, to help the poor, to open the first hospital for poor women. *To be the first woman doctor.* And Elizabeth Blackwell was strong enough to make every one of those dreams come true.